Jesus on Death Row

Jesus on Death Row

An Adaptation of the Gospel of Matthew

Rev. Jeff Hood

WIPF & STOCK · Eugene, Oregon

JESUS ON DEATH ROW
An Adaptation of the Gospel of Matthew

Copyright © 2016 Jeff Hood. All rights reserved. Except for brief quotations in critical publications or reviews, no part of this book may be reproduced in any manner without prior written permission from the publisher. Write: Permissions, Wipf and Stock Publishers, 199 W. 8th Ave., Suite 3, Eugene, OR 97401.

Wipf & Stock
An Imprint of Wipf and Stock Publishers
199 W. 8th Ave., Suite 3
Eugene, OR 97401

www.wipfandstock.com

PAPERBACK ISBN: 978-1-5326-1259-6
HARDCOVER ISBN: 978-1-5326-1261-9

Manufactured in the U.S.A.   NOVEMBER 29, 2016

For Will Speer, My Teacher on Death Row

1.

Jesus the Messiah descended from a long line of oppressed people. For twelve generations, Jesus' family struggled to survive. The story of Jesus was born into flesh in Harris County, Texas.

Mary was embarrassed to be pregnant. Not knowing how she got pregnant or even how Joseph would respond, Mary tried to hide the changes in her body. When the child started to show, Joseph asked Mary what was going on. Not wanting to lie, Mary declared that she was pregnant by the Holy Spirit. Joseph was furious and planned to never talk to her again. Running away in deep pain and anger, Joseph collapsed in an alley. Exhausted from crying and shaking over the loss of his one true love, Joseph fell into a deep sleep.

Joseph didn't know whether he was dreaming or not when an angel appeared to him and declared, "Come on man. Do you honestly think Mary was sleeping around? Go and take her as your wife. God put the child there for a reason. The child will go by Jesus and will save all people from their sins." These events took place in accordance with the words of a prophet, "It will be hard to believe, but a virgin will have a son. When the child is born, everyone will call him Emmanuel or the God who is with us." Joseph woke up and wondered about his sanity. When he realized that he was of sound mind, Joseph married Mary. The couple didn't have sex the whole pregnancy and the baby was born. The family proudly called him Jesus.

2.

Rolling in by bus from the East Coast, wise nuns arrived to Texas and asked, "Where is this child that was revealed to us in prayer to be the Messiah? We saw his star in the sky." When the Governor heard this, he was frightened that oppressed people would rise up together and overthrow his unjust system. Quickly, he brought the wise nuns in and confirmed the information. Scrambling, the Governor left and spoke with his closest advisors. Everyone gathered agreed, the child was a threat that must be eliminated.

The Governor brought the wise nuns back in and encouraged, "Go and find the child. When you do, please send word back. We want to celebrate his birth." Increasingly suspicious, the wise nuns left and followed the star. Not long after they arrived in Harris County, the wise nuns saw the star stopped over a housing project. The wise nuns raced into the apartment to behold Mary with her child. Slapping tambourines and cheering, the wise nuns worshipped at the feet of the child. The wise nuns opened their suitcases and offered beautiful stones and precious metals from the East Coast as gifts. Bright lights in their dreams warned them to not return anywhere close to where the Governor was. The wise nuns got back on the bus and quietly returned to their home.

The Governor was aggressive toward oppressed folks and the people in Jesus' neighborhood had had enough. Nobody knew when the next tragedy was about to go down. With violence everywhere, God appeared to Joseph in a dream and said, "Take your child to Mexico and remain there until I tell you to come back." Joseph packed everything and the family was off. The journey across the desert was difficult. After many days, Joseph, Mary and Jesus crossed the Mexican border and began to live undocumented in Mexico. This was to fulfill what was spoken by God through the prophet, "Out of Mexico I have called my son."

When the Governor realized the wise nuns tricked him, he became enraged. Declaring martial law in Harris County, the Governor proceeded to destroy every opportunity for advancement that any young oppressed men might have and ordered the police to harass them at every turn. "Shoot at the slightest provocation!" the Governor ordered. Lives were destroyed daily. This fulfilled the prophecy of Jeremiah, "Voices were wailing in lamentation and mothers wept for the lose of their children, because they are no more."

Many years later, the Governor died in a fit of rage. God appeared to Joseph and told him, "Get up and take Jesus and Mary back to Harris County. The Governor is dead." Packing up, the family started to travel through the desert. Journeying back into the United States was more difficult than leaving it.

Customs and Border Patrol agents were everywhere. None of the group had enough water to drink and each of them fell down exhausted on multiple occasions. If it weren't for Mary pushing the family along, they would have died. When Joseph heard who the new Governor was, he became afraid to go home. God assured him that he would keep the family safe. When the family arrived in Harris County, Mary suggested that they settle in Houston. The family made their home in Houston, so that what had been spoken through the prophets would be fulfilled, "The child will be called a Houstonian."

Many years after the family returned to Harris County, Jesus was sharing wine with others at a wedding party when a couple was shot and killed. Although there was no evidence or witnesses linking him to the crime, the District Attorney decided Jesus fired the shots and filed capital murder charges. Jesus' family had no money for counsel. To sway the jury, the District Attorney repeatedly called for vengeance and blood.

While his public defender slept throughout the trial, Jesus was found guilty and sentenced to death. Until the date of execution arrived, Jesus would sit in solitary confinement on the Polunsky Unit or Texas' Death Row.

3.

John the Baptist appeared in a cell on the pod and loudly proclaimed, "Repent! The realm of God is upon us!" John was the one that Isaiah spoke about when he shouted, "The one crying out in the pod: Prepare the way of God, make the paths straight."

John only ate health food and refused to eat any of the food served on the row. People from all over the country wrote to him, many believed him to have special spiritual powers. After the writers repented of their sin, John would splash water on a card, include instructions to rub it on their forehead and mail it to them for their baptism.

When the guards walked by, John screamed out, "You brood of vipers! Who warned you to flee from the wrath to come? Bear fruit worthy of repentance. You don't get a pass to do evil because of your position; God is the one who makes justice not you. Every tree that does not bear good fruit will be chopped down and thrown into the fire!"

"I try to baptize you with water for repentance, but one who is more powerful than I is coming; I am not worthy to stoop down and slip off his sandals. He will baptize with the Holy Spirit and fire. He will gather all the wheat and toss the chaff into the unquenchable fire."

Then Jesus arrived on the pod from Harris County. Upon arrival, Jesus asked for John's baptism. Thinking he wasn't worthy to baptize Jesus, John quarreled. Jesus replied, "Let it be so, for I need to be an example to the others." John consented. Through passing notes, the two planned to do the baptism as Jesus walked by John's cell the next day. The hour came for Jesus to be taken outside for recreation and John tossed Jesus the water card as he walked by his cell. When

Jesus rubbed the water card on his forehead, the ceiling of the Polunsky Unit opened up and the Spirit of God descended on him in the form of a dove. A voice from heaven spoke and said, "This is my beloved Son, with whom I am well pleased."

4.

The guards could not believe what happened. Everyone was afraid of Jesus. Deciding to place him on a higher level of punishment, Jesus was put in a padded solitary room and not allowed to leave for forty days and forty nights. While there, Jesus fasted and prayed. The great tempter came to him and said, "If you are the Son of God then make food appear." Jesus answered, "One does not live by food alone, but by the very words that proceed out of the mouth of God."

The devil took him to the top of the Texas State Capital and said, "If you are the Son of God, then jump off. For it is written, God will command angels to keep you from hitting the pavement." Jesus replied, "It is written, do not put the Lord your God to the test."

The devil then took Jesus to the top of Mt. Everest and showed him the splendor of all the nations of the world and said, "If you will worship me, I will give you all of these nations and your freedom." Jesus snapped back, "Away with you Satan! For it is written, worship and serve God alone." Jesus woke up in the padded room and couldn't tell what had actually happened. He had a strange sense that angels were with him.

John's execution date grew closer and Jesus decided to do whatever it took to get out of the padded room. When he eventually was allowed to return to his cell, Jesus passed through multiple other pods and what the prophet Isaiah spoke was fulfilled, "He will pass through multiple pods- those who sit in darkness see a great light, and for those who sit in the shadow of dawn...light will dawn."

From that time forward, Jesus proclaimed, "Repent, for the realm of God is here."

Looking across from his cell, Jesus encountered two brothers named Peter and Andrew who used to be shrimpers on the coast and declared, "Follow me, and I will make you shrimpers of people." Immediately, the brothers decided to become Jesus' disciples. On the other side of the pod, two more brothers named James and John called out to Jesus and they became disciples too.

Jesus and his disciples started sending out letters proclaiming the good news of God and offering prayer to cure all the ailments of the people. When people miraculously started to become well, Jesus became famous and everyone started sending him letters asking for prayers of healing. Letters started to arrive from all over the world. Jesus empowered many others to heal and proclaim the good news.

5.

When he saw how many people were interested, Jesus spent time writing his thoughts and convictions down from his cell. Upon finishing the writing, Jesus sent them out.

Jesus declared,

"Blessed are the depressed, for the realm of God belongs to them.
Blessed are those who grieve alone, for they will be comforted.
Blessed are the generous, for they will inherit the earth.
Blessed are those who demand justice, for they will be filled.
Blessed are the merciful, for they will be shown mercy.
Blessed are the pure in heart, for they will see God.
Blessed are the peacemakers, for they will be called children of God.

Blessed are those who are persecuted for doing the right thing, for the realm of God belongs to them.

Blessed are you when people revile and persecute you and utter all kinds of evil against you because of me. Your reward in heaven will be great, for in the same way they persecuted the prophets before you.

You are the salt packets of the earth. You bring the flavor. If you toss out the few salt packets you have then where is the flavor going to come from? If you waste the salt, then how will it be good for anything?

You are the light of the world. You cannot hide the light of a sprawling city. No one covers up the small light they have. When I let my light shine, it gives light to the whole cell. In the same way, let your light shine and brighten areas of darkness, so that people might see God.

Do not think I have come to overthrow the law. I have come that the law might be made full. For truly I tell you, there will come a time when all is made right and there will be no need for any laws. Whoever oppresses will be called least and the oppressed will be the most in the realm of God. For I tell you, unless your righteousness exceeds that of the clergy and politicians, you will not enter the realm of God as you are.

People say don't kill, but if you are angry with someone then you are just as guilty as if you killed them. If you insult someone, then you are liable to the community. If you curse at people, then you are in danger of hell. Imagine if these were the rules everyone lived by? When you start to do good works, don't continue until you are reconciled to those you hate or that hate you. If you are thinking about suing someone or someone is going to sue you, settle before you get to court. Who wants to be stuck in hate or court?

People say don't cheat. But I say don't cheat with your eyes. If your body causes you to hurt your self or other people then correct it. For it is better to correct the body than to hurt your self or everyone around you.

Marriage is meant to be permanent. Divorce and remarriage sucks the life out of all involved. If you have to get divorced, don't keep on getting married over and over again.

Don't take a bunch of oaths. Just do the right thing. Let your yes be yes and your no be no.

When someone oppresses you, turn the other cheek. If someone sues you, then give them what you have. If anyone forces you to walk a mile, then do two. Give to everyone who begs or asks to borrow.

Love your enemies and pray for those who persecute you. Follow the way of God, God loves and takes care of everyone the same. For if you love those who hate you, then you will change their hearts and change the world. If you only love those who love you, then you will be doing the minimum and the minimum never amounts to much. Follow God and try to be perfect like God.

6.

"Don't show off. If you are going to be generous, then simply do it and don't expect a big reward and accolades. When you can, do well by people in secret. God will know what you are up to.

Don't stand up and pray just for everyone to see you. Go to quiet places and pray. God will meet you in those secret places.

When you pray, don't just use a bunch of words to show off. Give your heart to God. God knows what is coming before you ask God.

Pray like this:

'Our God who is there
blessed be your name
Your realm grow on here
Your will be done

unrevealed as it is revealed
Give us this day our daily food
And forgive us our oppressions,
as we forgive all who incarcerate us.
Do not let us be consumed in times of trial,
but deliver us from evil.'

What you forgive will be forgiven of you and what you don't forgive will not be forgiven of you.

When you fast, do not let anyone know that you are fasting. Wash up and try to look like you are not fasting. God will see it and that is all that counts.

Do not store up things here. Even if I was interested, I don't have much room in my cell. Do justice and make peace so that you will sow fulfillment in God's realm. For what you value is where your heart is.

The eye is the keeper of the body. If your eye is healthy, then your body will be full of light. If your eye is full of darkness, then no light will be able to get into your body. If the light in you is darkness, then how great is your darkness!

No one can serve two masters! Either you will love God and hate things or you will love things and hate God. You cannot serve both.

I sit on death row and have found what it means to live past worry. Learn not to worry about your life, what you will eat, what you will drink, how your body looks or what you will wear. Is life not more than all of these frivolous things? Look at the birds of the air! God takes care of them. Do you not think that you are as valuable as the birds? Can you add anything to your life by worrying? Consider the grass of the field. Does God not clothe the fields in splendor? Do you think that God will fail to clothe you? Have faith! Don't spend your life worrying about things! God knows you need all of these things. Seek God first and all of these things will be added unto you. Do not worry about tomorrow. Today has enough troubles of it's own.

7.

"Do not judge! God will judge you by the same measure that you judge others. Don't point out the particle in the eye of a friend when you have a pole stinking out of your own. Don't you dare try to take the particle out of your friend's eye when you can't maneuver with a pole in your own eye. Take out the pole in your own eye and then you will be able to help others.

Do not give your pearls to pigs. They will trample them and turn and maul you!

Ask and you will get it. Seek and you will find. Knock and the door will be open unto you. For everyone who asks receives, everyone that searches finds and everyone who knocks will find the door open for them. Is there anyone who could give a stone when a loaf of bread is asked for? If a child asks you for fish sticks, would you give them a snake? If you would do the right thing in these circumstances, can you imagine how much more God will do for you?

Do unto others as you would have them do unto you.

Enter through the hard way. The easy way leads to destruction. The hard way teaches you to live life as God intended.

You will know whether people are false prophets or not by their fruits. Good trees bear good fruits and bad trees bear bad fruits. You will know them by their fruit.

Seek me. Don't seek anything else. Don't deceive your self into thinking that you are calling on me when you are not.

Everyone who hears these words and acts upon them will be like the walls of this prison. Come hell or high water, nobody is getting out. They build prisons strong to hold people in. Build your faith equally as strong.

When Jesus finished saying these things everyone was astonished."

8.

Not long after Jesus got done writing down his teachings, he was told he had a visit. When he arrived to the visitation booth escorted by three guards with shotguns, there was a man sitting there with inflamed sores all over his body. Picking up the phone, the man spoke into the receiver: "You can make me well if you want to." Jesus sent a spirit of healing through the cord and everyone in the visitation realized that the man was made well. The guards didn't know what to do and quickly took Jesus back to his cell.

Later in the month, one of the guards quietly approached Jesus. "One of my dearest friends has been struck with cancer. Can you heal her by declaring her well?" she tearfully requested. 'Wow!" replied Jesus, "I have never seen this type of faith." After some meditation, Jesus declared, "It is finished." When the guard arrived back at her locker, a message awaited her on her phone that said her friend was cancer free. According to the time stamp, her friend was healed the very moment that Jesus prayed.

One of his disciples in the pod slid Jesus a picture of his mother-in-law and said that he was told that she was sick in bed with fever. Jesus rubbed on the picture in prayer and made her well. On the pod, there were many evil people. Jesus cast out demons and healed as many as he could. These actions fulfilled the words of the prophet, "He took our infirmities and bore our diseases."

When people began to see and hear about what Jesus was doing, thousands of people wanted to correspond and follow him. One wrote, "I will follow you wherever you go!" Jesus replied, "I am sitting on death row. You need to come and visit to know what it means to follow." The gentleman replied, "I must first bury my father." Jesus answered strongly, "Come here and let the dead bury the dead."

There was a tornado about to hit the Polunksy Unit. Everyone on the pod thought that they were going to die. Jesus was asleep. His fellow inmates screamed for Jesus to save them. Half asleep, Jesus pointed out the window and demanded the weather calm. Immediately, the tornado was no more. Both the guards and inmates were amazed, remarking, "What type of man is this, that even a tornado would obey him?"

A few weeks later, two new inmates were brought to the Row. Within a few seconds, Jesus realized that the two were possessed and tormented by demons. The two shouted at Jesus, "What do you want with us Son of God? Are you here to torment us?" There was a large group of horses feeding in the field. The two demons asked to be thrown into the horses. Jesus replied, "Go!" The herd of horses galloped away. The two tormented men were now calm. Everyone continued to be amazed and frightened by these occurrences. Thinking his cell might be giving him some strange powers, the guards asked for Jesus to be moved a few cells down.

9.

Jesus moved a few cells down the Row.

During a time of visitation one day, children wheeled an angry and bitter paralyzed man to Jesus' booth. When Jesus felt their faith, he said to the paralytic, "Take heart, your sins are forgiven." Then some of the other inmates who were having visits remarked, "That dude really is nuts." Jesus perceived their murmurs and said, "Why do you think evil in your hearts? Is it easier to say 'Your sins are forgiven,' or to say 'Stand up and walk?' But so that you might know that I have authority to do it all, sir, stand up and walk." The gentleman was overcome with joy and got out of his chair to dance around. When the rest of the visitation room saw it, they were filled with awe and started celebrating the majesty of the moment. The guards were angered by the whole spectacle and quickly cleared the room.

While Jesus was being moved back to his cell, he saw an evil man named Matthew and said, "Follow me." From that day forth, Matthew did good and followed Jesus.

During dinner, Jesus talked to Matthew across the pod. The guards couldn't believe that someone who declared to be so religious like Jesus would associate with Matthew. When Jesus heard the talk, he said, "Those who are well have no need for a physician, but the sick need help. Go and learn what this means, 'I desire mercy, not sacrifice.' For I have come to be with sinners."

The disciples of John in a few pods over sent word, saying, "Why do we have to fast and your disciples don't?" Jesus said, "No one should mourn while I am here. The day will come when I am taken away, and then fasting will be appropriate. No one fixes a rip in their prison jumpsuit with a preshrunk patch before they wash it, for the patch would pull away as the fabric shrunk and the tear would be made worse. Neither is soda put in a bottle and shaken up, for it will burst and ruin everything in sight!"

While he was ruminating about these things with the guys on the pod, Jesus opened a letter from a prominent pastor that read, "My daughter has just died, but say the words and I know that she will live." Jesus asked the rest of the pod to pray before reading further. During their prayer, one disciple shouted out, "Jesus, I am having a vision of a woman who has been suffering from terrible hemorrhages for the last twelve years. She is begging you to heal her." Jesus shouted back, "Tell her, your faith has made you well." Jesus returned to prayer over the pastor's dead daughter. "I think she is just sleeping," Jesus shouted out. The disciples laughed at Jesus, until the ceiling opened up and they all saw a vision of the girl getting up out of the coffin at the funeral home. The miraculous occurrence was known throughout Texas and many very afraid.

Two blind men from another part of the prison sent word that they wanted to be healed. Jesus sent back a question, "Do you believe I am able to do this?" "Jesus, we wouldn't have asked you if we didn't believe with all of our hearts that you could do it," the blind men sent word back. "Let it be done according to your faith. Go to the bathroom, dip your fingers into the water and rub your eyes, " Jesus wrote. The men experienced healing exactly as they were told and spread the news of their new vision throughout the prison and beyond.

One of the guards had a demon that made him unable to speak. Jesus called the demon out of the guard and he started speaking immediately. Everyone in the prison was amazed and consistently said, "Nothing like this has ever happened around here!" Those guards and inmates that refused to believe in the love of Jesus replied, "Only the ruler of demons can cast out demons."

Jesus continued to heal and preach the good news of love. With compassion for everyone he encountered, Jesus collected followers. Looking around the pod and writing to others, Jesus consistently commented, "The harvest is plentiful, but the workers are few, God wants us to go out and collect the harvest."

10.

Jesus gave authority to his twelve disciples on the Row to cast out unclean spirits and cure every sickness and disease. Unfortunately, Jesus already knew that one would betray him.

The twelve were given instructions: "Proclaim that God is here with us. Cure the sick, raise the dead, cleanse cancer and cast out demons. Don't charge anything for anything. You will be taken care of. Whoever writes or visits, encounter them with generosity and decipher what they need to be set free. If anyone does not listen to your words, shake off the dust of your feet and get out. Those folks will realize the error of their ways on judgment day."

"You will be like sheep among wolves, be wise as serpents and innocent as doves. Beware of the religious people, they will make all kinds of false accusations against you and try to destroy you. Because of me, you will be drug before governors, parole boards and judges to give testimony. Do not worry about what to say, for I will give you the words to speak. The Spirit of God will speak through you. Remember, you will be betrayed and hated because of my name. But the one who endures to the end will be saved. When you are persecuted, just keep going."

"No disciple is over the teacher, follow me. Those who tell the truth are always maligned."

"Do not be afraid; for there is nothing that is covered up that will not be revealed, and nothing secret that will not become known. What I tell you in the dark, speak out in the light; and what you hear whispered, proclaim it loudly. Do not fear anyone. For they can only kill the body and cannot kill the soul. Remain loyal to the God that knows all and loves all. Do not be afraid, you are as valuable as anything."

"Everyone who acknowledges me on death row, I will acknowledge before God; but whoever or whatever part of them that denies me on death row, I will deny before God."

"I do not come to create spaces that are peaceful, I have come to push into and create dangerous spaces of love and justice. I will set family members against each other in a battle for truth and one's primary foes will often be in their own household. You must love me more than family. Truth and love are greater than the connection of blood. Those who think that they have found their life will lose it, and those who give their life to protecting and working to free me and others who are oppressed will find it."

"Whoever welcomes you welcomes me, and whoever welcomes me welcomes the one that sent me. Welcome prophets so that you might know where to go next. Welcome the righteous so that you might know how to become righteous. Whoever gives to those in need will never lose their reward."

11.

Once Jesus finished instructing the twelve, he told them to start proclaiming the message.

When John heard what Jesus was doing, he sent a question through his disciples, "Are you the one we have been waiting for?" Jesus answered, "Go and tell John what you hear and see: the blind see, the crippled walk, those with disease are cleansed, the deaf hear, the dead are given life, and the poor hear good news. Blessed are those who take no offense to such actions."

Upon writing to John's disciples, Jesus started to share about John: "Why is everyone so interested in John? Do you care because you think he is a prophet? John is more than a prophet. This is the one about whom it is written, 'See, I am sending my messenger ahead of you, who will prepare your way before you.' There is no one else born of women greater than John, yet the least are still greater than the greatest. From the birth of John the Baptist until now we have suffered violence, and the violent will take it back through love. For all the prophets prophesied about John before he came. Let anyone with ears listen!"

"What will I compare this generation? It is like children saying, 'We rhymed in the streets for you and you did not dance; we cried and you did not mourn.' John did not come eating and drinking. You said he had a demon. I came eating and drinking. You said I was a glutton and drunkard, a friend of nasty vile sinful people. Yet wisdom is vindicated by deeds."

Jesus started to rebuke the cities that would not change. "Woe to you, Dallas! Woe to you, Fort Worth! Woe to you, Denton! Woe to you, Texarkana! Woe to you, Lubbock! Woe to you, El Paso! Woe to you, Galveston! Woe to you, San Antonio! If the letters written to you had been written to Marfa, they would have repented long ago. On the day of judgment, it will be much more tolerable for Marfa than you. And you, Austin, will you be exalted to God? No, your solutions will be thrown to hell. For if the horrible laws passed within you have condemned you."

"I thank God that the truths of love and justice are hidden from the wise and revealed to infants. It is the gracious will of God. All things are granted to me by God; and no one knows me except God and anyone I reveal my self too."

"Come to me, all who are depressed and burned out, and I will give you rest. Take my cares upon you, and learn from me; for I am gentle and humble in heart, and you will find rest for your souls. For my cares are easy, and my burden is light."

12.

The disciples kept eating many snacks from the vending machines in the visitation room. One of the guards remarked, "All your disciples eat is junk food." Jesus replied, "When my disciples are hungry let them feast. Do you know what it means when I say, 'I desire mercy not rules?' Stop condemning the innocent and assisting in the demise of the guilty. For I am tired of talking about food."

Going back to his cell, Jesus started to pray. In a vision, a man with a withered hand appeared to him. The man's hand was withered from fighting others. Jesus struggled to decipher whether the man would return to fighting if he healed his hand. Upon realizing that grace is still stronger than the future possibility of sin, Jesus said, "Stretch out your hand!" The man stretched out his hand and it was restored. When the man went to the news media and shared what happened in a vision with Jesus, the authorities started to conspire about how to get Jesus executed faster.

When Jesus found out about this, he grew more and more resolute in his cell. More and more people started to write to him and he cured all who sought healing. Jesus asked everyone to keep it quiet. The actions of Jesus fulfilled the words of Isaiah: "Here is my servant, that I chose, my beloved, with whom my soul is well pleased. I will put my Spirit upon him, and he will proclaim justice to everyone. He will not wrangle or cry aloud, nor will anyone hear his voice in the streets. He will not stop until he brings justice to victory. And in his name all people will hope."

The guards brought Jesus an especially unruly prisoner who was also blind and mute. Realizing that his behavior was due to the stress of his conditions, Jesus put his hands on the prisoner's head. The prisoner immediately could see and hear.

Word of what happened spread to the entire prison and people excitedly declared, "Can this be God in the flesh?" Those in charge of the prison and their higher ups quickly dismissed what happened, "Jesus is just an evil magician and false prophet." Jesus knew what they were saying and remarked for all to hear, "Evil and righteousness cannot mix. Why would I heal someone in the name of evil? Where have you been to help this man? Whoever is not with me is against me, and whoever does not gather with me scatters. Blasphemy against righteousness cannot be maintained in this life or the next."

"Trees are known by their fruit. Bad trees produce bad fruit and good trees produce good fruit. You are a bunch of snakes! How can anyone who is evil speak good things? For out of the abundance of the heart the mouth speaks. The good person brings good things out of a good treasure and the evil person brings evil things out of an evil treasure. Every careless word will be discarded on judgment day. By your words you will be justified and by your words you will be condemned."

Quietly, the warden and administration of the jail said to Jesus, "We want to see one more sign from you." But he replied quickly, "You evil people! You have had signs and there are signs right in front of you!"

"When unclean spirits come out of a person, they wander around looking for a resting place, but they can find none. Then they try to go back from where they came from. When they arrive back, they find there original space empty, swept and put in order. Then they go back and get more unclean spirits, and they enter and live there. The space is worse off than it was before they came out of the person in the first place. This is how it is with those evil people who keep refusing to believe. They just keep collecting evil."

While he was still speaking, the guards informed him that he had a visit from his mother and brothers. Jesus replied, "Who are my mother and brothers?" And pointing to his disciples, "Here are my mother and brothers! For whoever follows God is my brother and sister and mother combined."

13.

Later in the afternoon, Jesus looked out his cell window. While he was looking, letters started to pile up in his cell and all of his disciples were interested in talking. Jesus had to retreat to his bed just to have enough room to breathe. Jesus started to tell his disciples many things in parables.

"There was farmer who planted some seeds. Some seeds fell on the pavement. The birds swooped down and ate them. Other seeds fell on gravel, where they had just a little soil and they sprang up quickly, since there was no depth to the soil. When the sun rose, the plants were scorched due to their lack of roots. Other seeds fell amongst the grass spurs, and the spurs grew and choked them out. Other seeds fell on fertile soil and brought forth huge amounts of corn. Let anyone with ears listen!"

The disciples were curious about why Jesus kept speaking in parables. He replied, "I am giving you the secrets of God. To those who have, more will be given and they will have in abundance; but from those who have nothing, even what they have will be taken away. The reason I speak in parables is to open hearts, minds and ears that are closed to normal ways of teaching. This is to fulfill the prophecy of Isaiah: 'You will listen, but never understand, and you will look, but never perceive. For the hearts of people have grown dull, and their ears hard of hearing, and they have shut their eyes; so that they might not look with their eyes, and listen with their ears, and understand with their heart and turn-and I would heal them.' But blessed are those eyes that see and ears that hear. Many have longed to see what you see and never saw it and hear what you hear but never heard it."

"Hear the parable of the farmer. When anyone hears the words of God and does not understand it, the evil comes and snatches away what is planted in the heart; this is what was planted on the path. As for what is planted on rocky ground, this is the one who hears the words and immediately receives it with joy; yet such a person has no root, but endures only for a while, and when trouble or persecution arises on account of the word, that person immediately falls away. As for what was planted among thorn, this is the one who hears the words, but the cares of the world and the lure of wealth choke the words, and they yield nothing. But as for what was planted on good soil, this is the one who hears the words and understands them, who indeed bears fruit and yields a tremendous amount of corn."

Jesus put before them another parable: "God's realm may be compared to someone who planted good seed in their field; but while everybody slept, an enemy came and planted weeds among the corn, and then escaped into the night. When the stalks came up and bore corn, the weeds also appeared. The farm workers came and said, 'Did you not plant good seed in your field? Where did the weeds come from?' The farm owner answered, 'One of my enemies must have done this.' The farm workers replied, 'Do you want us to rip out all the weeds?' The owner replied, 'No, for in ripping out the weeds you will damage the corn. Let both grow until the harvest and then we will separate the weeds from the corn. We will burn all the weeds and keep all the corn.'"

Then, Jesus shared another parable: "The realm of God is like a mustard seed that someone took and planted in a field; it is the smallest of all seeds, but when it grows it is the greatest of shrubs and becomes a tree, so that the birds of the air come and make their homes on the branches."

Jesus also added, "The realm of God is like cookie dough that is cooked until it makes a soft delicious batch of cookies."

Through a diverse use of parables, Jesus educated and awoke all who would listen. This is to fulfill what the prophet said: "I will open my mouth to speak in parables; I will proclaim what has been hidden from the foundation of the world."

Then he stopped preaching, went deep into his cell and laid down on his bunk. The disciples in the cells closest to him whispered and said, "Explain to us the parable of the weeds of the field." Jesus answered, "The Son of God plants the good seed in the field of the world. The good seeds are the children of the realm of God. The bad seeds come from the evil one. The devil is a farmer too. The separation and division is the harvest at the end of the age. The angels will be doing the reaping. The weeds will be burned in the fire. The corn will be gathered up. The Son of God will cleanse the realm and throw all sin and evil into the fire. The righteous will shine like the sun. Let anyone with ears listen!"

"The realm of God is like buried treasure, which someone dug up and hid; then in their joy they go and sell all that they have and buy the field."

"The realm of God is like a merchant in search of fine pearls, in finding the one pearl of his dreams, he went and sold all that he had and bought it."

"Again, the realm of God is like a net that was thrown into the sea and caught every kind of fish; when it was full, they drew it in and took it to the beach. The fishermen separated the good fish from the bad. This is what it will be like at the end of the age. The angels are going to separate good from evil. The evil will be burned off."

"Do you get it?" They whispered, "Yes." "Every writer from the realm of God is like the person who brings every treasure they have in their house outside and puts it on display." When Jesus finished explaining the parables, he quickly went to sleep in his bunk.

When Jesus woke up the next morning, he received word from Houston that everyone was incredibly critical of a piece in the newspaper that called him a religious teacher and prophet. "Where does this murderer get off thinking he has any religious wisdom or power? Is this not the truck driver's son? Mary is his mother right? Don't his sisters still live here? Don't his brothers live here too? Where is he getting all this from? Jesus is a good for nothing murderer! He's an animal not a religious teacher! We've all known this about him since he was a kid!" The entire city was deeply offended by Jesus. In a letter to the editor, Jesus responded, "Religious teachers and prophets are without honor in their hometown." Because of their unbelief, only a few people were healed in Houston.

14.

The Governor heard reports about Jesus; and he said to his advisors, "This is John the Baptist; he has been raised from the dead, and he has been reincarnated in Jesus." For the Governor had arrested John, shackled him and put him in solitary confinement on account of his constant criticisms of the many injustices of Texas. Though the Governor wanted to execute him, he feared the masses, for many people regarded John as a prophet. When the Governor's birthday came, there was a performance at the state capitol. The Governor loved a male dancer so much that he promised him whatever he wanted in Texas. Having previously been scorned by John, the dancer asked for his execution. The Governor went up to his office and ordered it done. The body of John was brought up from Huntsville to his house for everyone to see. The disciples of John picked up the body from the back of the mansion and buried it outside of Austin. Many of the disciples drove all night to Livingston to be able to visit Jesus and tell him what happened.

After being told about John, Jesus retreated to his cell and refused to get out of bed. All of Jesus' disciples kept calling for him and refused to eat until he responded. The disciples did not let up and Jesus took compassion on them. The disciples declared, "It is late and we have not eaten for days. We are about to call the guard and beg him to bring us some food." Jesus replied, "That is not necessary. What do we have here on the pod?" The disciples replied, "a bag of chips, a piece of cake, a soda and half of a peanut butter sandwich." Everyone slid what he had to Jesus. Taking the items, Jesus blessed them and started to pass them out. Through miraculous multiplication, everyone on the pod ate until they were full and there was plenty left over.

Jesus went back into his cell to pray alone. When the early morning arrived, a terrible storm battered the pod. Lightening opened up a hole in the roof and water started to fill up the jail. Everyone was terrified. The guards and the prisoners called out to Jesus. Walking through the wall of his cell, Jesus stood in the middle of the pod. "He really is a ghost, " cried out the guards. But Jesus responded, "Take heart, it is I; do not be afraid."

Peter answered him, "Jesus, if it is truly you, command me to walk through the wall of my cell." He said, "Come!" So Peter started walking toward Jesus in full stride. When he passed through the wall, Peter became frightened and the wall started to overcome him. He cried out, "Save me!" Jesus reached out his hand and pulled him through, saying, "You of little faith, why did you doubt?" When they returned through the walls to their cells, the storm, hole and water were gone. Everyone in the pod was remarking, "This truly is the Son of God."

When the day of visitation arrived, people recognized Jesus and asked for healing. Letters poured in asking for a piece of something of his so that they too might be healed. Everyone who asked for healing from Jesus was healed.

15.

The Bishops and Pastors started to come to Livingston from Austin to visit Jesus on death row and said: "Why do you break religious traditions? You do not speak about God in the prescribed ways." He answered them, "And why do you talk about God without any concern for injustice? For God said, 'Love the stranger amongst you.' You do not care about all the immigrants in this state who have nothing. You want to take whatever they have and deport them. So, for the sake of your religious traditions, you make the word of God void. You hypocrites! Isaiah prophesied rightly about you when he said: 'These people honor me with their lips, but their hearts are far from me; in vain they worship me, teaching human selfishness as doctrines.'"

Then he wrote to his disciples, "Listen! It is not what goes into the mouth that defiles a person, but it is what comes out of a mouth that defiles." The disciples wrote back and said, "Do you know that our Bishops and Pastors are taking offense to this statement?" Jesus responded, "Every religious movement that God did not plant will be uprooted. Leave them alone. They are blind guides in the world. If one blind person leads another, then they will both fall into the pit." After Jesus read what he wrote aloud, Peter shouted from across the way, "What does that even mean?" Jesus replied, "I don't see how you could still not get it. Do you not see that what you eat goes through your stomach and into the sewer? What comes out of the mouth comes from the heart and defiles. Out of the heart comes murder, selfishness, stealing, anger, hate and assault. These are what defile and imprison us, but to not say a prayer correctly or read the right Bible does not defile."

Annoyed and tired, Jesus retreated to his bunk and fell asleep. The guards awoke Jesus a few hours later and informed him he had a visitor. While he was visiting with one of his disciples from Lubbock, a woman in the visitation room started shouting, "Have mercy on me Jesus, my daughter is tormented by a demon of materialism." But he did not answer. The disciple asked Jesus to silence her. Finally, he answered, "I was sent to prophesy to the people of Texas." But she came and begged at the glass, "Lord, help me!" Jesus answered, "It is not fair to take food intended for Texans and throw it to someone from France." She remained persistent and replied, "Yet even the dogs get some of the crumbs that fall from the table of the teacher." Then Jesus answered her, "Woman, great is your faith! Let it be done for you as you wish." And the materialism immediately left her daughter.

After Jesus left the visitation room, he journeyed back to his cell and climbed into his bed. Everyone in the pod held up letters from people who were sick and in need of help. With one wave of Jesus' hand over the letters, the abused, the lame, the maimed, the blind, the mute, the angry, the hateful, the sick and many others that the letters represented were healed.

Jesus put all of the letters from people who were sick at his feet and healed them as well. Guards and other staff started to come to him and ask him to heal their sicknesses and wounds. People around the world were shocked, when all of a sudden their loved ones could walk, speak, talk and function. Everyone praised the name of Jesus from Death Row.

Early one morning, Jesus opened up a letter from a disciple who was helping undocumented immigrants. The disciple said that he was housing nearly four thousand undocumented immigrants and their families and had no means to feed all of them. In a letter, Jesus pronounced a blessing over his disciple's refrigerator and told him to start passing out the food. Miraculously, nearly ten thousand undocumented immigrants ate until they were full that day. The disciple photographed the miraculous occurrence and sent a picture to Jesus. From that day forward, the disciple never worried about food again.

16.

The Bishops and Pastors arrived once again to test Jesus. "Show us a sign from heaven that you are truly the Son of God!" the group demanded. Jesus answered, "In the evening, you say, 'the sky is red and beautiful.' In the morning, you say, 'It will be stormy today for the sky is red.' You know how to interpret the appearance of the sky, but you don't know how to interpret the times. You ask for a sign when the sign is right in front of you!" Jesus retreated to the back of his cell and refused to speak to them any longer.

Later, as the meal trays were being passed out. Jesus told the disciples, "Beware of the false stale bread of the Bishops and Pastors." The disciples remarked to each other, "Does Jesus not like the communion bread that they send down here?" Growing frustrated, Jesus replied, "Why are you talking about bread? Do you still not perceive? Do you not remember all the miracles? How could you fail to see that I am not speaking about bread? Beware of the false stale bread of the Bishops and Pastors!" Then they realized that Jesus was talking about the false teachings of the Bishops and the Pastors.

One day on the pod, Jesus asked the disciples, "Who do people say that the Son of Man is?" The disciples said, "Some say John the Baptist, others Elijah, and still others Dr. Martin Luther King, Mother Teresa or Gandhi." He said to them, "But who do you say that I am?" Peter replied, "You are the Messiah! The Son of the living God." And Jesus replied, "Blessed are you Peter, son of Jonah! For flesh and blood has not revealed this to you, but God did. Peter you are the rock upon which I will build my church and the gates of hell will not overcome it. I am giving you the keys to the realm of God. Whatever you bind on earth will be bound in the realm and whatever you loose on earth will be loosed in the realm." In addition to those on the pod, Jesus repeated the message in letters and told everyone to not to tell anyone that he was the Messiah.

Jesus started to let his disciples know that he would be executed in Huntsville and be raised on the third day. Peter whispered to Jesus, "This will never happen to you! We will never let you get executed." Jesus replied, "Get behind me Satan! You are considering only human things not the divine."

Then Jesus told his disciples, "If anyone wants to be my follower, let them deny themselves and take up the device of their execution and follow me. For those who want to save their life will lose it, and those who lose their lives for my sake will find it. For what will it profit someone if they gain the whole world but forfeit their soul? What would anyone give in exchange for their soul?"

The Son of Man is coming with God to repay everyone for what they have done. There are some of you who will not taste death before you see the Son of Man coming out of the realm of God.

17.

Late one night, Jesus whispered to Peter, James and John to come with him and he transported them to the top of the prison. James was afraid of the guards, but Jesus assured him that no one could see him. In an instant, Jesus was transfigured before them. His face shone like the sun, and his clothes became dazzling white. Suddenly, Moses, Elijah, Dr. King and Mother Teresa appeared and started talking to Jesus. Peter got happy and declared, "Jesus, it is good for us to be here; if you wish, I will make five dwellings for you and our guests." While he was still speaking, a bright light boomed down, "This is my beloved Son; in whom I am well pleased. Listen to him!" When the disciples heard this, they collapsed to the roof of the prison overcome with fear. But Jesus came and touched them, saying, "Get up and do not be afraid." And when they looked up, they saw no one except Jesus alone.

Upon transporting them back into their cells, Jesus ordered them not to tell anyone about what happened until he was raised from the dead. And the disciples replied, "Why do the Bishops and Pastors uplift the names and lives of ancient and modern saints?" Jesus replied, "They would rather talk about them than live like them. God was present in all of the saints, but the religious leaders refused to live like them and most often persecuted them. The Son of Man is about to suffer the same fate." The disciples understood the parallels to the story of John the Baptist.

During visitation, one of the guards approached Jesus and said, "Have mercy on my son. He is an epileptic and suffers terribly. Numerous times, he has been seriously hurt while seizing. I asked your disciples to help, but they couldn't." Jesus replied, "How much longer must I be here and listen to this mess? How much longer must I put up with all of this unbelief? Bring the boy to me." Later that day, Jesus rebuked the demon of sickness and the boy was cured before their very eyes. The disciples privately asked, "Why couldn't we cast out the demon?" Jesus replied, "Because you have little faith. If you had faith the size of a mustard seed, you could walk through walls unassisted. Nothing would be impossible for you."

Back in the pod, Jesus said, "I will be betrayed and executed. Then, I will arise on the third day." All of the disciples were greatly distressed.

Prison officials came to Peter and said, "Why does your teacher refuse to pay a tithe to the church?" He replied, "Jesus does not want to support the many injustices of institutional churches." Later, Jesus asked Peter, "Should you take tithes from innocent children or from others who are complicit in the evils perpetuated by the institutional church?" Peter replied, "From others." Jesus said to him, "Then the children are free. However, so that we pay our tithe and be free of the burden of explanation. Go to your toilet. You will find a fish inside. Open the mouth of the fish and pull the gold coin out. Take that and mail it to a religious institution that is resisting war."

18.

The disciples whispered to Jesus and asked, "Who will be the greatest in the realm of God?" Pulling out a picture of the child of one of his disciples, Jesus said, "Unless you change and become like this little child, you will never enter the realm of God. Whoever loves purely and humbly like this little child is the greatest in the realm of God. Whoever welcomes such a child in my name welcomes me."

"If any of you do evil to this child, it would be better for you to be drowned in the sea. Woe to the stumbling blocks! The times are tempting and evil, but woe to those who put out blocks to stumble over."

"If your hand or foot causes you to stumble, cut it off and throw it away; it is better to embrace God with the evil parts of you gone than not to embrace God at all. If your eye causes you to sin, cut it out and toss it away; it is better for the evil parts of you to be burned up than for all of you to not to embrace God."

"Do not despise any of these little ones around you, for I tell you that their angels continually see the face of God. What do you think? If a shepherd has a hundred sheep and one gets lost, would she not leave the rest in the field to go find the lost one? If she finds it, she will rejoice more over finding the one that was lost than over the ninety-nine that never ran away. God does not want anyone to be lost and will search for the lost until God finds them. God gets what God wants."

"If someone in the community sins against you, go and point out the offense to the member while you are alone. If the member listens, then you have regained a friend. But if you are not listened to, take one or two others along with you, so that every word will be confirmed by the evidence of two or three witnesses. If the member refuses to listen to them, tell it to the community; and if the offender refuses to listen even to the community, let such a one be murderer to you. Whatever you bind on this earth will be bound in the realm of God, and whatever you let go of on this earth will be let go of in the realm of God. If two of you agree on anything on this earth, God will do it for you. Whenever two or three are gathered in my name, I am there amongst you."

Then Peter whispered from the cell across the way, "How often should we forgive someone? As many as seven times?" Jesus replied, "Not seven times, but seventy-seven times."

"The realm of God is similar to the landowner who decides he wants to free his workers from their economic slavery and pay them back what he should have paid them to begin with. When he figured up everything, he brought the first worker in and gave him ten thousand dollars. The landowner begged for forgiveness. The worker took pity on him and decided to forgive him. Then the worker went back and demanded money that some of the other workers owed him. The workers didn't have it and the worker decided that he was going to take them to court. The workers begged him to not take him to court, yet the worker had no mercy on them. The landowner called the worker in and said, 'I was trying to make things right and you decide to go and oppress your fellow workers? Why did you not show them mercy? Those workers are going to make more money than you and will be your bosses from now on.' This is the way it is with God. Mercy will be shown to the ones who remain merciful and generous to all people in all spaces at all times."

19.

Before being confronted by some Bishops and Pastors, Jesus spent many peaceful days healing people, writing letters and enjoying multiple visits.

Pastor after Pastor and Bishop after Bishop wrote to test him, "Is it right for someone to get divorced?" Jesus responded, "People leave their parents to become one in marriage with someone else. God blesses such unions. What God has joined together, let no one separate." The Bishops and Pastors kept challenging Jesus with different scenarios and situations. Jesus replied, "Don't think about the scenarios and situations, do what you believe is perfect and what God has called you to do. Divorce is not the perfect way." The disciples replied, "This is a difficult teaching. Maybe it is better to not marry." Jesus remarked, "Marriage is complicated. Our ideas of marriage have excluded so many people. Sexuality and gender exist on spectrums. All people everywhere should simply cling to those that they love. Let anyone accept this who can."

In the visitation room, many children came to Jesus and asked for a blessing. The disciples couldn't believe how many children went up to the glass to be blessed by Jesus. Growing angry, the disciples tried to stop the kids. But Jesus said, "Let the little children come to me, and do not stop them; for the realm of God belongs to them." And he laid his hands on the glass to bless the children until the guards pulled him away to go back to his cell.

Not long after he got back, Jesus opened up a letter from a wealthy celebrity, "Dear Jesus. What do I have to do to inherit eternal life? Do I need to keep all the commandments? I feel like I already do. Any help you could provide would be appreciated. Thanks." Jesus chuckled a bit and then replied, "Give up all of your fame, sell everything you have and follow me." Later, Jesus heard the wealthy celebrity fainted upon opening the letter.

Jesus said to the disciples, "It will be hard for anyone who is wealthy or rich to get to the realm of God. Indeed, it is easier for a camel to go through the eye of a needle." The disciples were grieved and asked, "Who will be saved?" Jesus swiftly replied, "For human beings it is impossible, but with God all things are possible."

Peter questioned, "We have abandoned everything to follow you. What is in it for us?" Jesus replied, "You will join me in the realm of God where all will be renewed. There will be much to let go of between now and then. There the first will be last and the last will be first."

20.

"God is ready for you whenever you come to God. The time or the day doesn't matter. God has the grace to restore you whenever you arrive. God chooses to bestow grace on all. Those who come late will be treated as if they got there early. In the economy of God, the first will be last and the last will be first."

Before Jesus went out for a visitation, he turned to the disciples and said, "The time is coming when they will take me to Huntsville and I will be handed over to the corrupt authorities to be executed. The Bishops and Pastors will condemn me to death. I will be mocked and executed. On the third day, I will rise from the dead."

When Jesus arrived for his visit, the mother of some of his disciples came up to the glass to ask him a favor, "Will you declare that my two sons will sit next to your throne in the realm of God?" Jesus swiftly replied, "You do not know what you are asking. I don't think you are able to drink the cup I am about to drink." The woman replied, "We are able." Jesus declared, "You will drink the cup. The seats are God's to grant not mine."

When word got back to all the other disciples that the mother asked such a question, everyone was angry. Jesus calmed everyone down and said, "Whoever wishes to be great must become a servant. Whoever wishes to be first among you must become a slave. I did not come to be served but to serve. I have come to give my life as a ransom for many."

Secretly, guards brought two blind inmates to Jesus. The inmates cried out, "Jesus have mercy on us." Everyone told them to be quiet so that the administration wouldn't notice. Jesus asked, "What do you want me to do for you?" They both said, "Open our eyes." Moved with compassion, Jesus touched their eyes and made them well. Immediately, both regained sight and became followers of Jesus.

21.

One day after a visit, all of the inmates on death row and the guards banged things against the bars in celebration of Jesus. The shouts and cheers were deafening. This moment fulfilled the prophecy, "God is coming as the bars are banged and the hopelessly imprisoned shout for joy." Everyone leaned in to touch Jesus and laid paper beneath his feet in respect. "Hosanna! Hosanna in the highest! Hosanna!" they shouted. When Jesus arrived at his cell, the warden came down and asked, "What is all the commotion?" One by one people answered, "We are celebrating the prophet named Jesus."

Later that week, Jesus entered the visitation room and drove out all who were peddling drive-by religion. He said to them, "You don't care about these folks. You can't save souls with quick prayers. You save souls with love. Get out of here." Jesus cured the sick and the needy in the visitation room. The children started to shout, "Hosanna! Hosanna! Hosanna in the highest!" He left them and went back to his cell.

In the early morning, Jesus was hungry. Seeing a package of sweets in his cell, Jesus dove across the room. When he realized it was just an empty package, Jesus cursed the package. With two snaps of his fingers, Jesus made the package disappear. One of the disciples saw what happened and was amazed. "How did you do that?" he asked. Jesus replied, "If you have faith and do not doubt, not only will you make a package disappear, but you will be able to pick the mountain up and throw it into the sea. Whatever you ask for in prayer will be done."

One day, a couple of Bishops and Pastors came on the pod and were surprised when everyone told them that they believed in Jesus. "Who is this Jesus?" they said. "It is I," replied Jesus. "By what authority do you teach all of these folks all this stuff?"

they demanded. Jesus replied, "I will ask you a question. By what authority do you get to come on the pod and other Bishops and Pastors don't get to?" The Bishops and Pastors didn't know how to answer and said, "We don't know." Jesus replied, "Neither will I tell you by what authority I teach what I teach."

"An older mother had two sons. She asked both to help her move. One did and one didn't. Which one do you think did the will of the mother?" Jesus asked the disciples. In loud exclamation, they replied, "The first!" In response, Jesus explained the question, "The murderers on death row will get to the realm of God before everyone else. For you have believed and followed first. You met God in a strange place and refused to turn away."

"Maybe another story might make it clearer. A man owned a few homes and leased them out in a lawless country. When the time came to collect the rent, the man sent his assistant to collect from the tenants. But the tenants seized the assistant and killed her. Later, the man sent a group of police officers to get the rent. But the tenants seized the officers and killed them too. Finally, the man sent his oldest daughter and said, 'Surely, they will respect my daughter.' But when the tenants saw the daughter, they murmured amongst themselves, 'Here is the heir to these houses. If we kill him, then we will get the houses.' So they killed him in the backyard. What should the owner of the houses do with these tenants?" They replied to Jesus, "Put those piece of shit tenants to death and find renters that are not monsters."

Jesus replied, "Have you not read: 'The stone that was rejected has become the cornerstone?' The realm of God will be given to those who protect life. Those who destroy life will need to be destroyed and resurrected into life." When word got out to the prominent Bishops and Pastors in Texas, they knew he was talking about them. The religious leaders petitioned the Governor to have the execution date sped up. Fearing those who thought that Jesus was a prophet, they did everything in secret.

22.

Once more Jesus offered a story, "The realm of God may be compared to someone who gives a wedding for their daughter. The mother sent out attendants to gather everyone for the wedding, but no one would come. For a second time, the mother sent out attendants to get everyone who was invited and told them to tell them, "Everything is ready. I have a feast, a band and plenty of alcohol. Come to my daughter's wedding!" Everyone went away and joked about the wedding. Some even screamed and cursed at the attendants. The mother was enraged. Along with some loyal friends, the mother went out and told all of the people she invited that she was done with them. Then, the mother went out into the street and started inviting random homeless people. All sorts of people attended, some were good and some were bad. 'Those who are invited are not worthy to attend, but these folks are.' The wedding was filled with guests. There was one person who was making a particular disruption with crude sexual advances and ruining everyone's time. The mother went to him and kicked him out into the darkness of night. 'You will learn better,' she said. Many get the opportunity to come into the presence of God and few have done the work to be chosen."

The Bishops and Pastors plotted to entrap Jesus. Sending some of their members down to visit him, they said, "We know you are sincere. You teach in the way of God and love all people. So tell us this: Is it lawful to pay taxes to the government, or not?" Aware of their malice, Jesus replied, "Why are you testing me? If Obama is the president of the government then give to Obama what is Obama's and give to God what is God's. When they heard this, they were amazed."

Other religious leaders visited Jesus the same day and hastily declared there to be no such thing as resurrection. Then they thought they would really stump him, "If someone is married multiple times, then who will be husband or wife be in the realm of God?"

Jesus replied, "There is no marriage in the realm of God. As for the resurrection, God is not God of the dead. God is the God of the living. Do you want to be dead without God or alive with God?" The rest of the visitation room could not believe the answers that Jesus was giving.

After those religious leaders were silenced, more Bishops and Pastors went to death row and demanded to see Jesus. Upon entry onto the pod, the leaders pushed, "What is the greatest commandment?" Jesus replied, "Love God with all your heart, and with all your soul, and with all your mind. The second greatest is this: 'Love your neighbor as your self.' Everything rests on these two commandments."

After a pause, Jesus asked them, "Who do you think the Messiah is? Whose son is he?" They said, "He must be the Son of Dr. King." "What about the Son of Mary too?" Jesus probed. They shrugged. Jesus pushed them even further, "But if Dr. King and Mary call the Messiah God then how can he be their son?" The group left astonished and dumbfounded. No one asked any more questions.

23.

Jesus said to his disciples and mailed out in multiple letters the following words, "The Bishops and Pastors think they speak and act for God. Do what they say and not what they do. They condemn everyone and need to condemn their self. They love to be seen and heard. They love their places of honor and respect. They love it when people call them Bishops and Pastors, but these titles betray that there is one real Bishop and Pastor named God. The greatest among you will be your servant. All who exalt their self will be humbled, and all who humble themselves will be exalted."

"But woe to you Bishops and Pastors, you hypocrites! You lock people out of your churches and think that you are locking them away from God. You are not. I will find them. You cross land and sea to make a convert, and you are really just leading people to the same hell that you creating for your self."

"Woe to you, blind guides, who say, 'Look at what God has blessed me with.' You blind fools! God is with the poor not with your palatial sanctuaries and homes. Do you believe in God or stuff? Stop finding your worth in possessions!"

"Woe to you hypocrites! You raise money while neglecting the real work of peace and justice. You are neglecting the real work of God! You strain out a gnat but swallow a camel!"

"Woe to you Bishops and Pastors! You clean the outside of sanctuaries, but inside they are full of nasty greed and hate. Clean inside your self before you try to clean everyone else!"

"Woe to you liars! You are like whitewashed tombs. You look beautiful on the outside, but inside of you are the bones of the dead and all kinds of filth. You look righteous, but really you suck."

"Woe to you Bishops and Pastors. You build on the tombs of the prophets, but don't do anything they taught. You are murderers of truth! You snakes and vipers! How can you escape the hell that you have created for your self? You will keep doing injustice in the name of God. How many more will you execute? Those you murder will be the ones who save you. This will come in this generation."

"Austin, Austin, the city that kills the righteous prophets and gives political office and pastoral prestige to the vipers. How often I have tried to save you from death row, but you've always been unwilling. Your sanctuaries are desolate and meaningless, because you have refused to stand for justice. You will not see me again until you say, 'Blessed is Jesus who comes in the name of God.'"

24.

Later, as Jesus was coming back from shower, his disciples pointed to the infrastructure that imprisoned them. Jesus declared, "Not a stone will be left on top of another. This entire structure will be torn down and turned into a place of true love and justice."

When he was sitting in his cell, the disciples whispered, "When will this be? When will the end of the age come?" Jesus answered, "Many will come and claim to be the Messiah. Do not let them lead you astray! You will see wars happening and people will claim that they are not wars. Nation will rise against nation. Famines and earthquakes will fill the land. This will be the start of the birth pangs of the end."

"You will be handed over to be executed. You will be called monsters. People will hate you. False prophets will call it justice. The love of many will grow cold. The ones who endure to the end will be saved. This is the good news of Jesus. The message will be taken unto all the world and all will be made complete."

"When you see the destructive politician standing in Austin, as was prophesied by Daniel, then flee to the border. Get out as soon as possible. Do not delay. Woe to those who stay in Texas with children in those days! There will be great suffering caused by greed and hardened hearts. If anyone says, "Look! Here is the Messiah!" - do not believe it. False Bishops and Pastors will abound. The Son of Man will come in a flash and save everyone from the mess."

"The sun will be dark and the moon will give no light. Stars will fall from heaven and the powers will be shakened. The sign of the Son of Man will appear in the sky and all the tribes of earth will mourn their state. Then with a loud trumpet, God will restore the earth from one end unto the other."

"When the fig tree puts out leaves, you know that summer is near. So also when you see these things and feel God at the gates, you will know that the restoration is upon you. This generation will not pass away until all of these things have taken place. Heaven and earth will pass away, but the words of God will not pass away."

"No one knows the hour of the restoration. Everyone will be doing evil and God will restore what has been lost. People will be carrying evil and it will be taken from them. People will be thinking evil and the thought will disappear. People will be pushing evil and righteousness will push back. Those who are found immersed in evil will pass through the flame of purification unto righteousness. Be ready and do good for the Son of Man will come at an unexpected hour."

"Who is the faithful and wise lover? The partner went away and left his lover in charge of his home. Will he be able to take care of the house? Will he be found in the arms of another? Blessed is the lover that is found by his partner to be lovingly waiting when his partner gets home. Immediately, the two will get married and know that they are destined to be together. But the wicked lover will sneak off and sleep with as many others as they can. The partner will catch an early flight and come home to find his lover in bed with someone else. Enraged, the partner will cut off the relationship and let him go forever."

25.

"The realm of God will be like this. A group of ten guys waited up to meet the perfect man for their best friend. Five were being silly and five were being wise. The silly guys got drunk and were running around in circles. The wise guys stayed awake with their best friend and tried to encourage him that the perfect man was coming. As the hour grew late, the silly guys passed out and the wise guys grew drowsy. Then all of a sudden around 3am, the best friend exclaimed, 'Look! Here he comes! Come out to meet my man!' When the time for the wedding came, the best friend took the wise friends with him to the altar. When the silly friends tried to come into the ceremony, the best friend declined for them to be present. 'You couldn't even stay awake with me to meet him! You got drunk and made a mockery of an important moment for me,' the best friend said. Stay awake and don't get drunk, for you do not know the day or the hour when love will find you."

"It is like a woman who goes on a very long journey and entrusts her property to three friends. To each person she gave a job. She asked the first person to take care of the house. She asked the second person to take care of the swimming pool. She asked the third person to pick up the mail. Then she went away. The person in charge of the house rented it out and kept it up. The person in charge of the pool used it for parties and destroyed it. The person in charge of the mailbox used it to run a business. When the woman returned, she engaged each friend. The first person presented the woman with the keys to the house. The second person apologized for trashing the swimming pool. Though the third person was only in charge of the mailbox, they gave the woman a check for ten thousand dollars that they made from using the mailbox. Who do you think the woman was most pleased with? Who do you think the woman wanted to remain friends with? Who do you think the woman wanted to entrust her stuff to in the future? Those who sow greed and destruction will remain in the darkness of distrust."

"When I come to judge the nations. I will separate one from the other, the sheep on the right and the goats on the left. Then I will come to those on the right and declare, 'Come now into the realm of God and inherit all that I have prepared for you since the foundation of the world; for I was hungry and you gave me food, I was thirsty and you gave me something to drink, I was a stranger and you welcomed me, I was naked and you gave me clothing, I was sick and you took care of me, I was in prison or even in prison on death row and you visited me.' Then the righteous will answer, 'When was it that we saw you hungry and gave you food, or thirsty and gave you something to drink? And when was it that we saw you a stranger and welcomed you, or naked and gave you clothing? And when was it that we saw you sick or in prison or even in prison on death row and visited you?' Then I will answer them, 'Truly I tell you, just as you did it to the least of these you did it unto me.' Then I will say to those on my left, 'You never knew me; for I was hungry and you gave me no food, I was thirsty and you gave me nothing to drink, I was a stranger and you did not welcome me, naked and you did not give me clothing, sick and in prison or even in prison on death row and you did not visit me.' Then they will also answer, 'Lord, when was it that we saw you hungry or thirsty or a stranger or naked or sick or in prison or even in prison on death row, and did not take care of you?' Then I will answer them, 'Truly I tell you, just as you did not do it to one of the least of this, you did not do it unto me.' Those who neglected God will dwell in darkness and those who embrace God will dwell in light."

26.

When Jesus finished saying all of these things, he looked out at the disciples and said, "In two days we will celebrate the holidays, and then the Son of Man will be executed."

Bishops and Pastors conspired to force the Governor to go ahead and execute Jesus. Together they said, "We must have him executed quietly, or there might be a riot amongst the people."

While Jesus was visiting with a dear friend out in the visitation room, a woman brought a costly bottle of perfume and poured it on the glass to show her love for Jesus. When the disciples saw it, they were angry and said, "Why waste such expensive perfume? The money could have been given to the poor!" Jesus responded, "Why do you trouble this woman? The poor you will always have them with you, you will not always have me with you. This woman is preparing my body for execution and burial. Wherever my good news is proclaimed, everyone will remember this woman's deed."

Then one of the disciples, named Judas, wrote to the Bishops and Pastors and said, "What will you give me if I betray Jesus and give him to you?" The Bishops and Pastors promised him a move off of death row. Judas began the work to betray Jesus.

"How are we to have the holiday meal in here?" the disciples asked Jesus. "My time is drawing near. We will make quesadillas and slide them under the doors to each other. Begin the preparation on your hot pots."

When the evening came, the disciples started to slide quesadillas under their doors to each other. Jesus spoke up, "One of you is going to betray me." The disciples became greatly distressed and remarked to each other, "I would never betray him." Jesus answered, "The one who has a quesadilla in their mouth is the one who will betray me. I will accept my fate, but woe to the one that does the betraying. It would be better if he had not been born." Judas replied with a quesadilla in his mouth, "Surely it's not me?" Jesus replied, "It is as you say."

While the group was eating, Jesus picked up a piece of bread, and after blessing the bread he broke it, slid it to the disciples, and said, "Take, eat; this is my body." Then he took a cup, and after giving thanks he magically let it slide across the floor to each disciple, saying, "Suck the liquid off the floor, all of you; for this is my blood, which is poured out for you for the forgiveness of sins." You will not eat this bread or suck this wine until you partake with me in the realm of God.

On this night, you will all desert me. For it is written, "The sheep will scatter. But, I will meet you again after the resurrection." Peter shouted from his cell, "I will never desert you." Jesus replied, "Before the intercom dings three times, you will deny me three times." Peter assured Jesus, "Even if I must die, I will never deny you." All of the disciples said the same thing.

The lights went out and darkness covered the pod. Jesus instructed the disciples, "Sit in your cells and stay awake as I pray." Jesus instructed the disciples closest to him, I am grieved and know that the hour of execution is upon me. Remain with me and stay awake." Jesus threw himself on the cement and cried aloud, "If it is possible, please let this cup pass from me. Whatever the situation, I follow your will not mine." Then he called out to the disciples and found them sleeping. Screaming at Peter, Jesus said, "So you could not stay awake with me in this most difficult hour? Stay awake and resist temptation. The spirit is willing, but the flesh is weak." Then he went deep into his cell for the second time and prayed,

"If this cannot pass unless I do it, your will be done." The night was dark and snores of the disciples filled the pod. For the third time, Jesus retreated deep into his pod and said, "Please spare me God. Regardless, I will follow you no matter what." Then he came to the disciples for the last time and said, "Are you still sleeping? The hour has come. The rat is at hand."

While he was still speaking, Judas arrived with Bishops and Pastors and the Warden carrying guns and clubs. "Judas told us that you confessed unequivocally to the murder in Harris County. We granted him clemency for his honesty. Your time for execution has come," declared the Warden. When Jesus left his pod, Judas blew him a kiss. Jesus replied, "I still love you Judas. I know you did what you had to do." Then the group collectively grabbed Jesus and arrested him. Suddenly, one of the guards (who had secretly become a disciple of Jesus) pulled out his gun and shot one of the Bishops in the ear and blew it clean off. Jesus got one of his hands free and reached out and healed the ear of the guard. "Do you not think I could call down ten thousand angels to stop this? How would the scriptures be fulfilled if I did that?" questioned Jesus. At that hour, Jesus turned to the group that had come to force him to his execution and pushed, "Why have you come at night like this? My case has made national news and you seek to execute me while no one is watching?" The disciples deserted Jesus and trembled in fear at the back of their cells.

In the hearing room, the Pastor at the First Baptist Church came to Jesus surrounded by other Bishops and Pastors. The entire group wanted to execute Jesus and condemn him to hell. Looking to drum up more false testimony, the group brought in witness after witness to accuse Jesus of worshiping the devil. "I heard Jesus talking about evil people as if they would be saved. How can evil be saved without the savior uniting with evil?" remarked one witness. "I heard that Jesus was transformed into a ball of fire in front of the disciples. How can anyone be transformed into fire unless they are from the evil flames?" reasoned another witness. The Pastor of First Baptist stood up and declared, "Have you no reply?" Jesus remained silent. Then the Pastor of First Baptist said, "In the name of God, I command you to tell us if you are the Messiah!" Jesus replied, "It is as you say it is. The Son of Man is from God and will be seated at the right hand of God." The Pastor of First Baptist ripped his tie off and said, "You blasphemer! Why do we need anymore witnesses?" The group shouted out in unison, "Execute him! Send him to hell! Execute him! Send him to hell! Execute him! Send him to hell!" The group of Bishops and Pastors struck Jesus and spit in his face, "What are you going to do now you piece of shit?"

An official came to the cell of Peter and asked him, "Are you a follower of Jesus?" Peter quickly replied, "I don't even know the man!" A little while later a guard declared, "I know that you were one of Jesus' disciples!" Peter responded sharply, "I am telling you that we were never that close!" When a chaplain came by to minister to him about the lose of his friend Jesus, Peter responded, "I don't need no ministering. I really didn't know him!" At that very second, the intercom dinged three times. Peter remembered Jesus' words. Weeping bitterly, Peter crumpled to the ground.

27.

When morning came, Jesus was surprised to still be alive. The Bishops and Pastors met together to confer about his death. With the help of the Warden and the Sheriff, the group bound him up and took him to the Governor's Mansion. Arriving at a back entrance, the group got Jesus out and took him to the living room of the Governor.

Though Judas was free, he struggled to live with his self. Judas loved Jesus and missed him dearly, "What have I done to buy my freedom? I betrayed innocent blood. I can't live like this." Early that morning, Judas called the Bishops and Pastors to recant his testimony against Jesus. The group declined and told him to keep his mouth shut or they would tell everyone some of his darkest secrets. Repenting of what he had done and what he was about to do, Judas decided he could not live and committed suicide in an abandoned dusty field. There, Judas was buried and many still call the place a field of blood.

The Governor sarcastically asked Jesus, "Are you the son of God?" Jesus replied, "It is as you say." But when the Bishops and Pastors accused and questioned him, Jesus did not reply. Then the Governor said, "Do you not hear what all of these religious folks are saying against you?" Jesus gave no answer to any of the charges. The Governor could not believe Jesus would remain silent when he was standing before someone who could save his life.

There was a film festival in Austin and the Governor was looking to score some political points. Going on stage at the festival, the Governor told the crowd, "You will have the opportunity to release one prisoner. Your choices are Jesus or Barabbas?" As the men were being brought out on stage, the Governor's wife sent word that she dreamed about Jesus and not to harm him. Enraged at the potential the dream was sexual, the Governor led the crowd in their decision to release Barabbas instead of Jesus. Everyone screamed for Jesus to be executed. Realizing that hysteria was taking over, the Governor tried to wash his hands of what was about to happen before he handed Jesus over. The crowd wouldn't wait and officers grabbed Jesus to take him to the execution chamber.

Once he was in the car, the officers ripped off Jesus' clothes and mocked him all the way to Huntsville. Mile after mile, the officers beat Jesus relentlessly. Upon arrival at the execution chamber, Jesus could not walk. The officers ordered another inmate named Simon to carry Jesus to the camber. Inside, the officers offered Jesus a last meal. Refusing to participate in the charade, Jesus fasted and prayed. Two other prisoners were being held close to his cell. One of the prisoners taunted Jesus and said, "If you are truly the Son of God then get us out of here!" The other declared, "I know you don't deserve to die.

Remember me in paradise." Jesus decided to remember them both.

When the time came, Jesus was led to the execution chamber. With a loud voice, Jesus cried out, "My God, my God, why have you forsaken me?" Trembling with fear and unable to stand, the guards pulled Jesus to the chamber. "Dead man walking," shouted each guard who was present. Once strapped to the gurney, Jesus urinated all over his clothes. When asked if he had any final words, Jesus declared, "I am innocent." The execution did not take and Jesus suffered tremendously before he finally died 45 minutes later. Upon his death, a tremendous earthquake shook the chamber and a deep darkness overtook the land. In Austin, monuments inside the Texas State Capitol started to topple over and chairs were overturned in the legislative chambers. Tombs released the bodies of many worthy saints. When all of this took place, a great many people realized that Jesus truly was the Son of God. Everyone in the chamber was terrified and the body of Jesus was buried very quickly.

The officials remembered that Jesus said he would rise from the dead. To keep anyone from tampering with the body, the Governor decided to place four Texas Rangers at the tomb to keep it secure.

28.

Early on the third day, a hand came up out of the ground and grabbed the ankle of one of the Texas Rangers. Terrified, the Rangers scattered quickly. Later in the morning, Jesus' mother and two others went to the tomb to put flowers out. The group was surprised that no one was still there to guard it. Upon walking up, the group realized that the dirt was moved. Then, a great earthquake shook the group. A dazzling angel of God appeared and said, "Do not be afraid. Jesus has been raised from the dead. Go and tell the disciples. You will all meet him in Livingston." Driving as quickly as they could, the group raced to Livingston. Passing over a bridge, Jesus appeared to the group in the car. Swerving to a stop, the group listened as Jesus said, "Go tell my brothers that I am coming to see them."

While the group was on the way to Livingston, the Governor ordered no one to talk about what happened. The Bishops and

Pastors covered the whole thing up and pretended to not even know who Jesus was. Everyone protected their money and positions and said nothing. Later in the day, Jesus appeared to his disciples in Livingston and told them, "Go make disciples of the entire world, baptize them in the name of the Creator, Christ and Sustainer and teach them to obey all that I have shown you. I will be with you always, even unto the end." Jesus ascended through the roof to God. Before Texas executes them all, the disciples continue to work to share the message of Jesus with the world.

www.ingramcontent.com/pod-product-compliance
Lightning Source LLC
Chambersburg PA
CBHW070928160426
43193CB00011B/1617